A LITTLE HAPPIER

Also by Derren Brown

Tricks of the Mind
Portraits
Confessions of a Conjuror
Happy
Meet the People with Love

A
Little
Happier

NOTES FOR REASSURANCE

Derren Brown

BANTAM PRESS

TRANSWORLD PUBLISHERS

Penguin Random House, One Embassy Gardens, 8 Viaduct Gardens, London sw11 7bw

www.penguin.co.uk

Transworld is part of the Penguin Random House group of companies
whose addresses can be found at global.penguinrandomhouse.com

First published in Great Britain in 2020 by Bantam Press
an imprint of Transworld Publishers

A CIP catalogue record for this book
is available from the British Library.

ISBN 9781787634473

Typeset in 12/18.5pt Bembo Book MT
by Couper Street Type Co.
Printed and bound in Great Britain by Clays Ltd, Elcograf S.p.A.

Penguin Random House is committed to a sustainable
future for our business, our readers and our planet. This book
is made from Forest Stewardship Council® certified paper.

For the Little Piglace

CONTENTS

NONE OF THIS IS REAL

Happiness is perhaps the most elusive aspect of the human condition, although it masquerades as entirely straightforward. It seems as if it is something we should all have access to, and we are looked upon suspiciously if we don't possess it. Yet to chase happiness directly is a conspicuously self-defeating project.

This book presents a model for happiness that dates back over two thousand years, yet is pertinently modern. Many of the ideas here are in direct opposition to the tenets of the modern self-help industry, and most likely to our intuitions. Others may seem obvious, but in their cosy familiarity have lost much of their bite.

I'm going to set out a model discussed at greater length in my book *Happy*. If you've read that book, I hope this will serve as a handy reminder of the fundamental ideas; it is perhaps a little easier to dip into. If you haven't, I hope that once you have read this, the longer book might offer you a chance to explore the ideas here in more detail. The ancient model we are for the most part considering is Stoicism, which is perhaps the most effective approach to finding contentment that the human mind has conceived. No one school of thought should pretend to offer the answer to everything, but I do think Stoicism is of enormous use, whether we adopt it as a complete lifestyle or simply use it in doses where it can make our life a better, calmer, more robust experience. At points in our discussion I will talk about the potential drawbacks of Stoic philosophy and, throughout, embellish with other points that are not from their tradition but which I think are useful.

Let's begin with fiction. We live amongst an infinite

data source. There are limitless things we *could* think about, or *could* pay attention to. To process all this information would be an impossibility, so how do we reduce it to something manageable? We tell ourselves stories. Stories about how the world works. About what people want from us, how things should be, how we should be, what we have to offer, how we relate to the world. And these stories allow us to simplify a complex and messy environment into something we can navigate; something that feels predictable enough to allow us to move forward.

The nature of good stories is that they have neat beginnings, middles and ends; cause and effect are precisely delineated; characters are clearly cut. Stories supply us with meaning, but to do this, they have to exclude much awkward information and confusing nuance that would mess up the neat narrative arc. As we form these kinds of stories about the world, they tend to become enormously compelling, and we emotionally invest in many of them. We forget that they *are* just stories, and mistake them for self-evident truth. When we listen to a friend talk about an ongoing conflict in which she is involved, the chances are we will quietly sense there is another side to the story that is not being told. It's probably hard for *her* to see this, but if she could – if she could place her story alongside the stories of others and realise that her perspective is far from the whole truth – we sense it might help her with her frustration. Our scepticism about her limited world view would be affectionate on our part. We forget to apply this same fond doubt to our own tales of what's going on around us.

To offer an analogy from my normal job: imagine you're fooled by a magician. The magician is exploiting our story-forming urge to make us join up the dots in a way that suggests the impossible has happened. We know there is a rational explanation so we are caught in a conflict which might be fun, or annoying, depending on what we think of magic tricks. But we are being shown that, however carefully we have been watching, we have unwittingly excluded some vital information. Or maybe we've watched too carefully, and missed the bigger picture. Things are going on we don't know about. The story we have been cajoled into telling is compelling but clearly inaccurate.

Stories, it's been said, are things told in fire-lit clearings, surrounded by darkness. But all that darkness – the bigger picture – is rejected from the cosy scene, while we remain mesmerised by the comfort of the firelight. Our first step then is to recognise the existence of that mysterious, obscure world of information we're simply excluding. This is important, as monsters lurk in the dark. When we banish information from our story of the world, it has a tendency to grow powerful, and to come back and bite us. Consider all the aspects of our own identities that we dislike and try to expel from our story of who we are. Buried into our unconscious, they can come to own us, as they feed into our addictions, avoidances and repeated relationship problems.

Let's prepare to listen to our internal dialogues a little harder, and catch ourselves in the act of telling stories we mistake for the truth, in the way an affectionate friend might. We can start to look out for too-tidy narratives that reduce complex truth to simple patterns, like those everyday niggles that so-and-so *always* or *never* does such-and-such. Or the times we decide we are helpless, based on previous experience, and become unnecessarily paralysed in the present. Or when we seem to be mind-reading: deciding we know a person's motivations for doing things that annoy us. The times we quickly catastrophise, and live out an emergency when we don't need to. These are all examples of unhelpful stories: we have told ourselves a tale of what events mean and, in that certainty, are making ourselves feel in some way bad. But it wasn't the event or the person causing the problem, it was only the narration we provided. This book will show you ways of improving that storytelling as it affects your relationship with yourself, events and others.

We mistake the horizon we see for the parameters of the world.

BE WARY OF GOAL-SETTING

Faith healers use a clever trick: after they have exploited the pain-killing qualities of adrenalin and had some poor soul bounce around on stage to show she is 'healed', they often tell her to throw away her medication. Faith alone, they assure her and the crowd, will maintain the healing. If the problem returns, it is *her* fault for not having enough faith.

Of course, the adrenalin wears off and the problem inevitably reappears, and now this sufferer has nowhere to turn. In fact, she must add her own failure before God and her peers to her existing list of problems. The healer, meanwhile, has moved on to the next town.

The same cycle of self-blame is at work within the

story we are typically sold by the authors of self-help books. The importance of goal-setting, and how to ensure its success, fill their pages and have spilt into the accepted image of what an active and admirable life must look like. If we set our goals and believe in ourselves enough, the universe will provide. If it fails to do so (and this is sometimes implied, sometimes explicitly stated, as in Rhonda Byrne's *The Secret*), it isn't the universe's fault: it's ours, for not having enough belief. Most of the self-help industry is pinned on this lie.

Barbara Ehrenreich, in her book *Bright-Sided: How Positive Thinking is Undermining America*, traces the injunction to be positive above all else to Calvinism: a form of Protestantism with a particularly gruelling work ethic. Under Calvinism, constant labour and accompanying material success indicated that a person was one of God's elect. The fact that today many people feel guilty if they're not filling their time with work is traceable to this Puritan movement. Ascetic dedication to labour was a way of absolving the terror of damnation that was seen to hang over all of us. Dickens's Scrooge is a Calvinist figure.

Then, in the nineteenth century, the American New Thought Movement sprang up, partly in reaction against Calvinist teachings, emphasising that we could heal ourselves and become divine by rigorously controlling our mental state. It was an attempt to break away from organised religion, but as often happens with reactionary movements, it changed the variables while inheriting the underlying grammar of what came before. Thus it fetishised hard work, like its religious predecessor. We now take it for granted that we should be advancing ourselves with consistent goal-setting and moving forward in a fierce frenzy of self-belief. If we set our goals and work hard whilst maintaining complete faith in ourselves, we should succeed. Or so we expect.

But we don't need to feel like this. Goal-setting is all well and good for short-term ambitions like learning a language or passing a test. But to commit oneself to a goal that spreads over years is to invite all sorts of problems. Here are a few of them:

What happens when you achieve the goal? Then what? A friend was committed to building up a successful business and then selling it, in order to retire early. He immersed himself fully in the project, which spanned decades of his life. When he finally achieved the goal, he was shocked to find that he retired to a crushing sense of emptiness. It turned out that it was not the goal but the journey that had been important to him, and now it was over.

What have you missed in the meantime? We might pursue a goal to be a millionaire by a certain age but neglect our relationships in the process. And by the time we get there, who knows how our values will have changed? To make such a commitment in the naivety of youth is unlikely to serve us over time. We may climb a ladder only to realise at the top that we had it against the wrong wall.

What if you fail to reach it? Now you must add failure – and a sense of wasted time – to your list of problems.

Goal-setting fixates us on the future, and is closely related to the notion that there is a ladder of success we must climb. We choose our GCSEs at school based on the A Levels we think we must like, based on what we think we will want to do at university, based on what job we are aiming for, based on what promotions will be available … in order to reach … what? There *is* no final plateau that is reached: instead, we have relentlessly focused forward while life has slipped by and happened in the meantime. An alternative thought may be helpful: to be guided by a sense of what's enjoyable. I watch my beagle-basset sun herself by the window, then move to the concrete kitchen floor to cool down, then bury herself in her bed, then help herself to the sofa. This is a *horizontal* alternative for thinking about career, albeit one that leaves hairs everywhere. It allows us to respond to the stirrings of the soul rather more than one that locks us in for a decade or more to a specific image of progress. If we can maintain a kind of internal coherence, an infusion of this horizontal approach permits exploration and avoids the stagnancy and shackles imposed by an exclusively upward commitment. The more familiar *vertical* model is the echo of religious imagery (we read in the Bible of Jacob climbing a ladder to God). Its suspect promise of eventual salvation need not dictate our modern approach to work.

There is not going to be a point when it all comes together. So let's not waste our time: instead, arrange what we can to ensure the journey is enjoyable and meaningful. Alan Watts (who brought many Eastern ideas to the West) made the point that when we listen to a piece of music or read a book, we don't just skip to the end, where it all comes together. But in life, we fixate on endings. Perhaps, instead, life is more like a piece of music, and we are supposed to be dancing.

Treat your goals with scepticism, and keep them short-term, because they are based on the illusion that you can control the future. When you look back on your life, isn't it largely a series of false starts and meanderings? Hasn't luck (good or bad) played an enormous role? Do not be seduced by the heroic stories of business gurus who have committed themselves to a single vision of success, ignored the nay-sayers, and focused exclusively on what they believed against all the odds. They're just stories, too cute and cosy, told round firelight in a clearing. They read well in books, but they also present a perfect formula for failure. *Commit to a single-minded vision, ignore the nay-sayers, focus exclusively on what you believe*: the same mantras may lead to ruin as well as to triumph. Unfortunately for our sense of balance, failed businesspeople rarely write autobiographies.

WALK THE DIAGONAL

What, then, should we do with our aims and ambitions? If the pursuit of goals is common but unhelpful advice, what serves us better?

This cult of grail-seeking implies, in essence, that we can control Fate through the sheer potency of our self-belief. The Ancient Greeks would have laughed at our pride. Those tragedians would point us towards their rich dramatic works that expose this human tendency to over-inflate our abilities: our *hubris*. Words like 'Fate' or 'Fortune' are no longer popular: we have grown so self-assured in our ability to control our destiny that they have lost their potency.

We need to acknowledge mighty Fortune as a force in our lives. One day things will work out for us, and the next they won't. On that second day, it doesn't mean we've failed. It just means we are caught up in the natural to and fro of real life. How easy it is to blame ourselves, and revive an old story of being worthless, spineless, unlovable, or in some other way hopeless. If we believe that we can control our lives through self-belief, then of course we must be to blame when Fortune turns against us.

Here is a helpful alternative. Arthur Schopenhauer, the great German philosopher of life, offered it to us in the nineteenth century:

'Events and our chief aims can be in most cases compared to two forces that pull in different directions, their resultant diagonal being the course of our life.'

Imagine a graph, with 'Our Aims' represented by the vertical axis and 'Fortune' along the bottom. Our life travels in an $x=y$ diagonal that soars up and along that graph. If we look more closely, we'll see it isn't a straight line: it meanders above and below the true diagonal. Sometimes we are on top, and life is progressing as we wish. On other days, or in other years, it is not: Fortune throws its weight back at us. Like it or not, we snake across this line, enjoying the highs and suffering the lows. The optimism of modern self-help – the legacy of Puritanism and a nineteenth-century quasi-mystical movement – tries to convince us that we can force that line up and over to our side, making life yield to our wishes, that the universe will diligently provide. But then a recession strikes, or our house burns down, or a loved one receives a crushing diagnosis. We cannot escape the reality of the diagonal. So rather than fight it, the trick is to make our peace with it: to move in an easier accordance with Fate.

When Freud founded the talking therapy that would give rise to modern self-help, his aim was not to make people happy. It was to restore 'natural unhappiness'.

He saw this as a realistic but preferable alternative to the 'unnatural unhappiness' that plagued his patients. The goal was to bring us back to the balance of real life, where we find our never entirely satisfying meander along an $x=y$ diagonal. Donald Winnicott, an English psychoanalyst and paediatrician, later wrote in praise of the 'good enough' parent, who slowly disillusions her child, teaching them that life will not always provide. This supported the sound instincts of caregivers and amounts to another acknowledgement of our $x=y$ dynamic.

Schopenhauer saw our lives as a back-and-forth between the poles of pain and boredom. Pain calls us to action and persists if we don't respond to it. When we do, pleasure refuses to endure and quickly turns to boredom. Anything else would threaten survival, and thus we move forward. Again, that $x=y$. It's a pessimistic model, but in more recent times, the psychologist Mihaly Csikszentmihalyi has offered a similar dynamic as a template of how we achieve a state of 'flow' – the optimal state, in which we feel at our best. Whether we are surfing, playing chess, painting or performing, we can come to lose ourselves, and any sense of time, in a certain mood which is not quite happiness but where we are operating superlatively. In this flow state, the skills we employ match the challenges we face. If the skills are outweighed by the challenges, then we become anxious. If things are too easy, we grow bored. So along that softly zigzagging line that pulls between our personal power and that of life, we find a vibrant space to flourish. Although these short-lived periods are different from the push and pull between resources and challenges across a lifetime, we can note with less defeatism than Schopenhauer that life turns out to be an expanded form of our optimal state of flow.

We are dismissing the notion of a vertical line: represented by the ladder, which we forever try to ascend, ignoring the rest of life in the meantime. Equally, we have no wish to lie flat along the 'Fortune' axis and passively yield to every circumstance. We should try to steer our lives where we can, but when it takes hold of the wheel and adjusts our course, or throws in a devastating corrective, we need not blame ourselves. Our only fault lies in over-estimating our control over things.

Allow a place for Fortune. She turns out to be a crucial part of the game: an opponent who might become an easy companion.

OUR TERRIBLE JUDGEMENTS

The stories we tell sit between the world and our responses to it. Very little reaches us without being first embellished by our inner narrator, and what does quickly subsides. Channelled through stories, information takes root and forms our experience. But whatever moral compass our narrator uses to form those stories has been skewed. We estimate everything by our judgements, but take no care to ensure anything approaching accuracy in our measuring apparatus. Our vital tools for daily evaluation are hopelessly unreliable, idiosyncratic and fundamentally damaged. They are the only ones we have, and we are convinced they're in excellent working condition.

When we were young, we were handed a set of rules

about what was important and how we (small and helpless) relate to the world (big and powerful). That information came most likely from our parents, who would have had their *own* skewed information to work from. Carl Jung, the great psychoanalyst, said 'the greatest burden a child has to bear is the unlived life of its parents'. Consider that: we start with a warped vision of reality that we then carry through life. It informs the stories we live out each day, about who we are, our worth, other people and their motives. These are really hard stories to question, because they run so deep. They generally feel completely rational and normal. Our responses to the troubles we face, which sometimes baffle or frighten others, seem to us utterly in proportion to the events at hand. It's difficult to apply the same affectionate scepticism to our own stories that we do to those of our friends, or to notice how, in the same way, they are merely revealing the things about which our particular history has made us especially sensitive.

Although it seems very much as if events and people cause our problems, it is these stories we should be questioning. If you are sceptical that your judgements are to blame, and there is an ongoing issue which you insist is currently vexing you *directly*, consider this: could someone else react differently to it? Perhaps you even know someone who might? If you can imagine someone responding in a way at odds with yours, then *it is not the event that is having a direct effect on you*, it is only your judgement of it. And it is within our power to change these judgements.

It seems hard to imagine how we might effect such a change. Especially if we believe we are at the mercy of our passions, and that to try to change them through conscious effort is futile. But our emotions are more amenable to our more rational aspects than we tend to think. Consider how we might feel if our partner or dearest friend appeared to have no interest in our upcoming birthday. We'd most likely feel rejected. But if we were to find out she was organising a surprise party for us, our feelings would no doubt quickly change. Whether our heavy-heartedness yielded to sweet fondness or an augmented horror, new information would have had a direct and logical effect on our emotions. If we provide them with new information in the right way, our feelings are usually happy to listen.

This is not to suggest that our emotions are generally guided by our rational minds, in the way we might like to imagine. The relationship between the hot and cold aspects of our personalities has been a subject of much debate throughout the history of philosophy, and the legacy of the Greeks – particularly Aristotle – may be to have granted too much weight to our intellect. Most of the time our rational decision-making *feels* like it's in control, but in truth it is following the way our emotions are already leaning. Thus, when we are asked to do something we don't want to, we quickly come up with reasons to justify why we shouldn't. Sociologist Jonathan Haidt suggests the memorable metaphor of a rider thinking he's controlling an elephant. The latter, our unconscious mind (or we can think of it as our emotional 'side'), leans one way, and our rational, conscious mind (the rider) is brought along with it. In some ways this model is at odds with the thrust of Stoic thinking, which, like the cognitive-behavioural therapy that it has inspired, posits our decision-making processes coolly at the helm. I would suggest that the two are not incompatible. Certainly, if we are in a foul temper, it will be harder at first to implement Stoic techniques. In that sense we are at the mercy of our moods and gut responses. However, with time, there's no doubt that practice expedites the process, lowers the temperature, and palliates the seeming sovereignty of our passions. Indeed, establishing a healthier dialogue between the two realms is an ambition of most philosophical approaches to the considered life.

If our anxiety is a trapped, turbulent area of water, rational intervention of the sort we are considering can open up carefully plotted tributaries to guide it towards calmer places. Anxiety will generally prefer to follow those new paths, gently driven forward by the sense of relief which follows. It feels right.

When we are hurt, offended, upset or angry, we are – if not just hungry or tired – commonly feeling the echoes of the story of ourselves and the world we absorbed during childhood. If, little by little and despite our best intentions, we were made to feel in some ways unlovable, or perhaps convinced that others will try to control us, we will be especially sensitive to those reappearing scenarios as adults. And when they arrive, that cluster of energy is activated and we feel something like a panic, or we shut down, *as the world conforms to our deepest fears about it.* We will tend to experience a fight-or-flight response, this most likely depending on the prevailing atmosphere working upon us when we were young. An aggressive household may have taught us to fight back, to be alert for any sign of conflict and quickly rise to meet it.

Another may have left us feeling alienated and alone, so we withdraw. We are likely to have developed a fear of abandonment (perhaps convinced that people are constitutionally unfaithful and that partners will leave us) or of being overwhelmed (jealously defending our space, pulling away quickly from emotional pressures as they arise). Although these responses are overwrought, they are fatally familiar. And so we will recreate them throughout our lives: if we are committed to a belief that our partners will betray us, we will too quickly become suspicious and jealous, and drive them to other lovers. The lure of what is familiar dictates the structure of these stories, their unquestioned grammar of cause and effect, their lessons to be played out in our lives again and again. The repeated problems in our adult relationships tend to demonstrate how we look to recreate with each new partner what is familiar from our family ties. Our parents have left us a flawed prototype for life and love. I will discuss this troubled legacy later.

But frequently our anger and upset are frightened responses to the manner in which our feelings resonate with our history of analogous experiences.

Importantly, in accepting the vital role of our storytelling, we are not just blaming ourselves for our woes. The point is to learn a new robustness: *whatever happens to us need not affect our core unless we choose to let it.* Viktor Frankl, an Austrian psychiatrist who wrote an extraordinary memoir of his time in the concentration camps, found this to be the thought that allowed him to survive. His words from hell: 'Everything can be taken from a man but one thing: the last of the human freedoms – to choose one's attitude in any given set of circumstances, to choose one's way.'

The fictional rendering of the objective world into manageable, personal form is both the primary source of our trouble and the only authentic place to seek remedy. But how are we supposed to reconfigure these narratives that have us in their grip? Sometimes, being aware of their power is enough. We can practise being attentive to the kinds of stories we tell ourselves about the world and ourselves. But we are going to need some clear guidance as to how, in the heat of the moment, we might change them. So let's first consider where, specifically, we're hoping to head.

THE ANCIENT ART
OF TRANQUILLITY

We now have some basic understandings at our disposal. In terms of emotional health, there is wriggling space between the world and our reactions to it, and that leeway is formed by the stories we tell. Those stories are informed by our personal history, which brings with it a set of biases and clusters of sensitivity that give us anything other than a clear view of reality. Moreover, the world will always provide challenges and disappointments, and offer reasons for despair. Our existence is complex and messy, and only sometimes corresponds with our wishes. And it serves us to reassess how we accommodate those forces, rather than try to force them into submission.

I expect then, as we continue, that the ideas in this book will only sometimes be sustainable, and other times will feel out of reach. I am presenting a model which, in a world of complex relationships and responsibilities, may at times feel hard to put into practice. But trying it out as and when it's manageable will, I think, help build confidence. What at first can feel quite alien is often just a question of 'leaning into', trying new habits, noticing the results.

Let's muster a specificity about what we'd like to achieve. Part of our challenge is that, like the rainbow that symbolises it, happiness appears to have substance from a distance but recedes and wanes when we try to approach it. When we try to define happiness, we find that it slips through our fingers, and when we accumulate the things in life that we think will make us happier, we find that they don't, at least not for very long. Yet we persist in seeing it as a birthright, a *thing*, perhaps a thing that others have and we don't, or a reward that will arrive promptly when other events of our lives have been ticked off.

As we progress through these pages, we will assemble the components of a far more helpful and *concrete* model of happiness. It was constructed by the Ancient Greeks, who drew from the East, and then popularised during the Roman era. This is the model offered by Stoicism, a widespread school of thought that was very interested in what constituted the Good Life. When Christianity spread wide its golden fingers across the pagan world, Stoic thinking was either purloined or banned. Questions of what it was to live well were deemed to have been more than adequately answered by religion, and to question dogma was blasphemy. Now, in our less reverent times, we can engage in a little philosophical archaeology, and rediscover some of these ideas. Stoicism was born in a time of strife, and remains useful and disarmingly modern in our current world.

The Stoic preference was to develop a robust form of tranquillity, with which to face a world that presents us with disappointment and frustration. The Greeks called this tranquillity *ataraxia*. It is *the avoidance of disturbance*, of needless vexation and anxiety. This is a key point: we are switching our lens towards the negative. We are not chasing the thing we want directly: instead, we are looking at how we might *avoid* the obstacles that block our path. This change in tactic brings with it a surprising advantage: we can now begin to be more precise, to grasp our aims in a way that makes the project manageable, where trying to tackle happiness head on has only proved futile. Chased directly, it will elude us, but if we see it as a by-product, and decide to glimpse it only in the mirror, we might obtain it more easily than we think.

This is far from the modern image of happiness, which, alongside an explosion of pharmaceutical solutions available to the unhappy user, has become equatable with mere mood. It may feel like a mood change is all we require, but a thought experiment by philosopher Robert Nozick suggests otherwise. Imagine you had the opportunity to attach yourself to a machine that you could programme to give you whatever happy experiences you like for the rest of your life. Would you plug in? In reality, you would be stretched inert on a bed, perhaps turned by nurses, while your brain carried you to all sorts of happy places and gave you whatever experiences you liked. Would you substitute your life for this? Maybe it's tempting for a moment, but if you wouldn't do it, it's because you want something more than just a certain ongoing mood or experience. Somehow, we desire meaning, immersion – not just a feeling, however nice.

Anxiety has its place, and we will return to that theme. But for now let's continue with a model for circumventing it where it is needless, and gathering ourselves to a place of unruffled, open resilience. We can retain such a resource in our emotional arsenal;

we can practise it until it becomes part of us; we can, in our own time, let the cloudless restorative of tranquillity drip into our soul.

WHY ALMOST
EVERYTHING IS FINE

How, then, to gather up the disordered threads of our personal narratives and weave them into some unifying pattern? We seek to avoid disturbance, but how do we do so in a world that seems committed to impeding our every attempt to summon peace?

A common theme in science fiction and fantasy cinema is the wielding of control over external forces – think of *The* Force. Very often, the novice is faced with a conundrum when learning such a skill: to try *not* to try. Skywalker and others must attune themselves to something powerfully and eternally effortless in order to achieve a higher level of being. This notion has its roots in the harmonious Way of Taoism, which bled into early Stoicism. The first Stoics were from the East, which is why ideas of non-attachment, for example, are seen in both the Greek teachings and those of Buddhism. But the intellectual mode of the Stoics better suited our Western tastes than the mystical perspective, and thus Stoicism acted as a kind of holding ground for Eastern ideas, albeit re-worked in more a rational vocabulary. Most of us do not talk comfortably of people being holy or enlightened in the same way as other traditions might, but the Stoics do posit a semi-fictional sage who acts as an exemplar *nonpareil* of their way of thinking. The theme, however, is present across all these schools of thought: by moving in a more harmonious accordance with the flow of the universe, by relinquishing certain kinds of control, we elevate our existence and gain a form of quiet, ethereal power. It's an idea that one way or another has entranced those who seek the Good Life in either hemisphere.

As anyone who has tried to practise The Force in real life will attest, trying to move an object through telekinesis is frustrating and pointless. If anyone can do it, it's me, and when I tried it with a paperclip it barely shifted. Expending any effort trying to control something outside of your sphere of influence is an incontestable waste of time. Let's then consider the reverse formula as a means of *avoiding* frustration. *Don't try to control things that are* not *under your control.*

So far, so good. But what is not under our control? An easier question, if we revert to the positive phrasing, is: what *can* we control? And the answer becomes clear: we can control our thoughts and our actions. That's it. Controlling either of them may not always be easy, but they lie at least within our remit. They are things of which we are, to one degree or another, at least in charge.

Everything else is external to us, and therefore out of our control. Let's consider that self-evident but troubling fact. How other people behave, what they say, how they treat us, what they think is true: these things are not under our control. Neither are external outcomes, the results of our actions; much of the future and certainly the past; likewise, we wield no power over what the world ultimately makes available to us. Now, such matters may not be *completely* out of our control, and I will get to that in a moment. But here is the key manoeuvre: decide which side of the line a problem falls into. Is it something within the realm of your thoughts and actions? Or is it something external?

You are most likely to find it is something external. And if so, here is the second tactic: decide that *whatever is outside of your control is fine.*

That may take a bit of unpacking to sound acceptable. We are being asked to decide that the things we cannot control (the things external to us) are fine as they are. To do that, we need to believe the following fact: *If we decide the things out of our control are fine, nothing bad happens.* The verso of this, if it helps, is:

How would I make a situation I cannot control any better by pointlessly trying to control it?

Remember the previous chapter: our aim is to seek a robust tranquillity. For the purposes of this new stage we are discussing, let this be enough. In order to find external things satisfactory when they appear otherwise problematic, we can turn for assistance to the cognitive trick of confirmation bias.

When we read or hear an argument with which we don't agree, we instinctively look for things that *aren't* right and retain them as evidence for why we can disregard the argument. When we dismiss as ill-informed an article upholding a view we dislike, our rational mind has most likely been led by the gut instincts we already had in place. Conversely, if we are presented with an argument for a premise we *already agree with*, we will soak up every point of affirmation that bolsters the view we are in truth already committed to. In the first case, according to psychologist Tom Gilovich at Cornell University, we are asking ourselves, '*Must* I believe this?' and looking for any reason why we don't have to. In the second scenario, our key question is, '*Can* I believe this?', which biases us towards the slightest grounds for acceptance.

Now let's do the same with our purposes, and ask, in the face of a troubling situation: *How might this be fine?* How might it be fine that this person treats us disrespectfully? How might it be fine that I have lost something dear to me? That the world is moving in this direction? That my partner handles stress badly? That I am single yet again? How might these things actually be fine? We can ask the question, and let the answers arise from our depths, without force or goading. Sometimes they will come quickly, with a rush of relief. Other times they'll take a little longer.

Next, let's consider the rumblings you may have felt a few paragraphs back. Maybe the distinction between what is *in* versus *out* of our control sounded facile. We're not in control of anything outside of ourselves?

Then why bother trying to change anything? What about matters of social injustice? If we are to decide that everything external to us is agreeable as it is, how do we get ahead or correct evil as we see it? How might we get our story heard when our voice has been all but silenced? Is protest futile? Should we not try to change a broken system?

The answer is: *absolutely* we should, if we wish. Talk of tranquillity can make the Stoics sound like they were recommending complacency, compliance, or inaction. But the foremost Stoics were statesmen and politicians: the movers and shakers of their age. Marcus Aurelius, one of the great figures in Stoicism, ruled the Roman Empire during one of the most war-torn periods of history. His privately penned *Meditations* stands as a touching note to self by a philosopher-king trying to navigate the all-too-human pressures of life and office. We are not turning away from making change; we are merely minimising the hindrance of unnecessary disturbance and creating a fortified centre of calm. And an unruffled, more robust approach is only going to help us create any change we wish to see.

So how do we marry this 'it's fine' with, say, fighting prejudice and ignorance? The Stoics would still say: separate what is and what is not under your control. But now the uncoupling will take place within a sub-domain: what parts of creating change are under your control? *To fight your cause, to do your best to change the world*: these are under your control. These are your tasks, if you wish to take them up. However, strictly speaking, is it your job *to succeed*? It is not, for at that point, Fortune must step in. *To show others where they are ignorant*: that is a task you can choose to undertake. *If they choose to treat you with ignorance*: that is not your business, it is theirs. What you do, you can do with utmost conviction; what others do is for them. Separate your tasks from those of others, even if, which is likely, your aim is to have them behave differently. You can champion your cause, but to *commit* yourself to an outcome that may not arrive until a generation after you've left the Earth is going to cause you a bitterness that will impede your efforts. This is why the most effective civil rights protests throughout history have channelled raw anger into constructive measures. There is a time for anger, of course, and advantages in being shored up by an ideal, but they are not likely to get you far. Thus, it still helps us to separate what is ours and what is not, what we can control and what we cannot, and while we put energy into the former, we aim to treat the latter with whatever dignity and serenity we can find.

What then about personal, historical trauma? Is the suffering of childhood sexual abuse *fine*, because it is past and out of my control? Well, here the language is unhelpful, as 'fine' has connotations of 'excusable', which is clearly *not* the intention. However, consider what would happen if, after years of effective therapy, an adult survivor of such early horrors was for the first time able to comfortably move on with her life.

To reach such a point would be optimal, given what has gone before. The past would have lost much of its grip on the present. She might hope to learn ways of detaching from it, of putting history in its place, relinquishing its power in the here and now. The same hope for robust tranquillity is being articulated: things are now 'fine', 'manageable', 'comfortable' in the lived present.

We can practise asking this question, *How is this fine?*, with minor problems in life, and see what happens. Perhaps it's fine because how that person is acting does not need to affect us, and we do not need to change them. Or maybe it's OK because the world is full of stressed people, amongst whom we must count ourselves. Maybe we can be every bit as irrational and over-sensitive as they can: and when we are, we know we rarely mean anything by it. Maybe they don't either. Perhaps it's fine because we don't need to grant anything or anyone the power to diminish our self-worth. And our feelings, however overwhelming they may seem, are *things we have*: therefore *they cannot be us*; our self exists in a place outside of them. And if, for all that, it's really *not* fine, then what can we do within our thoughts and actions to remedy the situation or extricate ourselves from it?

We are pulling our centre of gravity in towards us. With purpose, we are loosening it from external areas where it has become tangled while we forgot to pay attention. We are gathering it back inside, where it belongs. Where is it otherwise? To connect it to ambition, Marcus Aurelius noted, is to tie it to what others say or do. To desire fame, for example, is to locate the source of our happiness in the thoughts of other people (namely, what they think of us). Self-indulgence is to attach it to what happens to us. Sanity, finally, is to securely fasten our well-being *to our own actions*.

If we do not come from a place of strength, we cannot offer much to ourselves or the world. Robust tranquillity, a gathered-in gravitational centre: these are the best starting points we can have upon which to base our behaviour. Emotions we put out into the world can emanate from a nucleus of strength or weakness. Love, born from brokenness, can grow to be as destructive as hate; kindness can be generous or manipulative. Always, we (and others) are served by first ensuring we have tended to our core, that we are not acting from deficiency. Unless every disturbance is going to throw us, every possibility of insult prove intolerable as our propensity for sensitivity proliferates and chokes us, then our efforts to alter aspects of the external world should come *after* we have first paid attention to the one thing we can actually change: ourselves.

THE SECRET FORMULA
FOR SUCCESS

Before continuing this notion of an attention-to-self, let me take further the notion of this 'Stoic fork' – the division of events into those in and those out of our control – and apply it to a specific context: success. The pursuit of success commonly correlates with our notions of happiness. Are we in control of our triumphs and prosperity? Again, we must distinguish between the parts under our control and those that are not. What then *is* under our control? Our *talent*, certainly. And the *energy* with which we get that talent noticed. To have all the talent but no ability to share it would leave us overlooked; to have all the self-promotional skills but nothing worthwhile to promote isn't going to get us far either.

All else is on the far side of that dividing line – that of the external – and need not bother us. Whether we get the call, the gig, the promotion, the job ... there will be a thousand reasons why these may or may not happen that have nothing to do with us. As we cannot control them, it's useful to make our peace with them. So the formula for success is Talent + Energy. My manager mentioned it many years ago, and only years later did I see how it resonated with the ideas of the Stoics.

Consider a game of tennis, in a valuable analogy offered by William Irvine in his work *A Guide to the Good Life: The Ancient Art of Stoic Joy*. If we play determined to win, and the other player turns out to be better than us, we will probably start to feel anxious. Our game will probably suffer. By trying to win, we are attempting to control something outside of our remit. On the other hand, consider what happens (and doesn't happen) if we aim instead to play *as well as we possibly can*. If our opponent starts to gain the upper hand, we need not feel like we're failing, because we are not. We feel less anxious than in the first scenario, which also means we can expect to play better. And a keen tennis player friend assures me this is good game advice.

In matters of success, we need only focus on developing our talent and energy: the twin poles of doing the best we can. If the job goes to someone else, great – *it was theirs*. This is particularly helpful in the uncertain world of performing. Actors might discover a healthy approach to auditions: Bryan Cranston has spoken of how it is not your job to get the job (which is out of your control), instead the task is only 'to create a compelling and interesting character that serves the text and to present it in the environment where your audition happens, and then you walk away'.

Focusing on talent and energy keeps us rooted in the present: fame and success are too early tangled with desire, which keeps them fettered to the ever-receding future. If your job offers the potential of happiness, it will be found in the journey, not at an end point that is ill defined, unknown, and never really quite arrives. So don't confuse fulfilment with fame. Keep your centre of gravity within. And, as a final note, beware the toxic blend of low self-esteem and grandiose self-regard known only to the truly damned.

ATTEND TO YOURSELF

The Stoics called their attention-to-self *prosoche* (as in 'pro-soccer'), and it captures their fundamental attitude. It distinguished them from the Epicureans: the prototypal-hippy garden-dwellers who aimed to take a simple joy in the natural pleasures of the moment. A pleasing premise, but they had no choice but to accept handouts in order to survive. The Stoics were by comparison far more engaged and characteristically resolute, actively finding ways to guard against any threat to tranquillity. We should also therefore bear in mind that a certain amount of tenacity is required if we are to continue this dialogue with ourselves and achieve the Stoic take on *ataraxia*. Tenacity, correctly understood, can be a gift rather than a chore. If we start off well using these ideas, and then mess up completely, *this is entirely permissible.* We can just remind ourselves of the project, note our newly discovered weak spot, and continue where we left off. The same thought will help the person giving up smoking: you might berate yourself for a guilty cigarette following three months of abstinence, and treat it as a failure, when in fact it is a resounding success. Fifteen a day to *one in three months.* Maybe six months later you'll have another. Seeing a slip as failure commonly makes us throw in the towel, when the key thing is to dismiss it with good humour, congratulate ourselves for what we have achieved, and keep going with the project.

Prosoche is making sure that we are remaining suitably in charge of ourselves. It is favouring the considered life: keeping an eye on our ways of being and values from an imaginary third-person perspective, and seeking an inner coherence. It is adopting the techniques in this book. This kind of attention helps us untether our centre of gravity from wherever it has drifted, and restore it to a point inside. It gives us distance from our negative emotional responses, which is often all we need to avoid being swept away by them. This kind of interior dialogue allows us to question our attachment to positive feelings too: other people's flattery and our fancy new purchases can feel nice, but we can aim for a healthy scepticism over attachment. By allowing this Stoic voice in our head to speak up and hold us to account, we can take some control over what we choose to assent to. And when we do feel bad, we have a wise interlocutor who can remind us of what is and what is not our task, and point us towards helpful solutions instead of the more familiar, unchecked nagging voice – that of our own history – which too often spirals us into ever-deepening gloom by focusing us on what we lack.

However, we must next turn to a reminder: the aim is not self-absorption. It is to pay attention to the development of one's personhood in such a way that one becomes more robust, more useful to one-self and, ultimately, to others. The modern maxim to 'own one's story' is so often a spur to impose our unconsidered fiction on others, identify proudly with our brokenness, and refuse to grow. But that is not the best experience of authorship we might wish for ourselves. Instead, let's consider the edges of our fiction by finding the truth in the perspectives we exclude; seek to heal our brokenness by affording ourselves the sustained compassionate attention we might lend a child; and finally, seek the discomfort of growth over the calcifying effects of security.

THE DANGERS OF
SELF-SUFFICIENCY

These Stoic maxims can sometimes seem to encourage an aloof detachment from others, as we decide to only take care of our own business and not let others have an effect upon our tranquillity. But I'm not sure that's quite what the Stoics intended, or indeed a helpful aim. There's no need to seek remoteness from the world. A useful metaphor the Stoics offer us is that of waves lashing against a rock, and the rock remaining steadfast despite the onslaught. But the philosopher Martha Nussbaum suggests that at times it may help us to prefer a picture of a pebble, rolling around with the edge of the tide. Or a rock that is porous, and lets the water flow through it. Moving in easier accordance with life and those who populate it is assisted by these notions of easy movement and porousness. To hold our centre within, while extending outwards into the lived world, is to discover a resonant new place for love.

The Stoics do not have much to say about love, other than how to avoid being hurt by it. But we must keep room for it as we fortify our centre, because then our love can come from strength, and through it we find meaning, and achieving a sense of meaning is another indirect means of finding happiness. Those who end their lives are not the merely unhappy: they are usually those who have lost all sense of meaning. *Purpose and value* – which are products of storytelling – mean more to us than mood. And likewise, our self is not something we retreat into; it is something that extends outwards into our relationships. In that sense, love truly holds us – our self – together. And this is an outward movement we should encourage, and all the more so alongside a philosophy which can, taken the wrong way, seem to advocate withdrawal.

In romantic relationships, growing less bothered by events that continue to upset a partner can, ironically, open the way to a treacherous new path. If you lean towards introversion, and are thus perhaps more constitutionally suited to the serenity of Stoicism, while your partner sees the world as a list of problems to fix, then your growing Stoic reserve may be a sticking point of frustration for them. They may feel, in the smiling face of your stolid repose, that they are not being heard. Sensitivity, rather than being expunged, will need to be fine-tuned: you may, for example, need to pretend to be angrier than you feel, and certainly resist an immediate attempt to assure them that all is well. Your growing sense of indifference to those things outside of your control, which constitute the external world, will need careful expression in company where people may care very much. Empathy remains hugely important.

Recently I was sitting in the lounge area of a hotel in Conwy, a small and achingly pretty Welsh town outside Llandudno. The doors had been thrown open as the day was very hot; I had come inside to write after desiccating outside in the sun for an hour. The patio was small and probably needed some planters to cut off the view of the adjoining car park. But scattered around the few brown and yellow tables were families and small groups, and every fifteen minutes a bell rang from a nearby church identifying the quarter-hour, which lent the scene an unexpectedly Tuscan air.

I watched a slim woman in a white dress and a floral bandanna pour tea for herself and her husband. Another couple adjusted the position of a chair for an elderly man I presumed to be the father of one of them. A chap in his early thirties took off his hat, sat back in his chair, and raised his face to the sun while his friend perused his phone. A poodle lay on its side in the sun, little curly legs outstretched. Two women chatted over white wine; the older one (whose face I could see) was about fifty, and evidently very attentive to the successful arrangement of her bobbed blonde hair each morning; she was showing off her tanned arms with a sleeveless black dress.

With the fine weather and occasional bell-tolls buttressing my appreciation, I suddenly felt a strong sense of delight in these people. Each had decided to put on *those* clothes this morning; to sit facing *that* way in the sun or shade; each expressed their affection for or ease with their companions in some different and touching way. Each was here, enjoying the same heat, sharing the same space; each, like the waitress who brought plates of risotto and crusted cod to her customers, was doing their very best to balance their responsibilities and desires and navigate their life as well as possible. Each personality seemed strikingly distinct; every choice of shorts, sandals or haircut was suddenly rendered *perfect* for them: a moving signifier of how that person wished to portray him- or herself to the rest of the world. Each piece of exhibited, unconscious body language was an affecting window into private motivations and the delicate ballet of the particular interactions in which they found themselves.

Perhaps it was just the sun, but some invisible barrier dissolved, and I felt an enormous affection for my fellow hotel guests – a feeling that brought a great sense of happiness. And sitting here now a week later in a small private library in Nottingham, watching a woman repeatedly wake herself up with her own farts, I again experience the flood of fond-feeling from that afternoon and extend it towards the venerable and unhurried bookworms who are scattered here around me; crumple-faced reminders of extraordinary lives being lived, right here, right now.

LOWER YOUR EXPECTATIONS

I once watched a wealthy restaurant owner, dining at his establishment with friends, bellow vile insults at his own waiter for bringing water at the wrong temperature. Presumably, he was trying to impress his guests, who were clearly ready to chew their fists from embarrassment. That failed attempt aside, it was a foul illustration of a particular madness that creeps in with success: we start to measure the world against our absurdly high assumptions.

This tendency is not only displayed by the rich, but it is most unpleasant in their case. A diva shouting down backstage staff for not adhering to her ludicrous dressing-room rider is a far worse sight to behold than a guy complaining about a cold pizza in a takeaway.

But we should learn from the diva, as her anger will feel as justified to her as our own does to us. What she can teach us is this: *our frustration amounts to proof of how unrealistic our expectations were.*

The Stoics were keen to have us remember, whenever we state our aims, to tack a qualifying 'if everything works out well' on the end. *Deo volente*: God willing. By reminding ourselves of the interplay of Fortune, we can plan for success and prepare for failure.

People will let us down. The contractor may have said he would be finished by the end of the month, but who said he would be able to keep his word? The lady from the call centre assured you she would make a note on your account, but who said she would actually do so, or that her note would reach the right eyes? We will be forever surrounded by errors, obstacles and incompetence. Thus it makes sense to hold back from committing ourselves, to await the capricious issue of events, know that our purpose may be strong but results will be uncertain. This won't come naturally to us, at least at first. We have to take a moment to do this: to remind ourselves of the Stoic reserve clause, that outcomes are always outside of our control.

Aim in this way for a persistent, quiet resolve in the face of adversity. Remember, we can continue with our efforts whilst remaining unconcerned with the outcome. Aim for success, but treat its arrival as a bonus. If it does not come, then remember that your true goal was only to try, *and in that you succeeded*.

'Do not seek to have events happen to you as you want them to,' said Epictetus, a great Stoic teacher, 'but instead *want them to happen as they do happen*, and your life will go well.'

Again, this can sound complacent. It need not be if we apply it therapeutically to those areas outside of our control where it is most needed. It may not be helpful language for a protest poster, or for rallying a revolution, but in many areas of life it is a useful antidote to our frantic, misjudged efforts to control what is happening around us. It can remind us to value what we already have, demand less of others, love more, deepen our resources of satisfaction and tranquillity.

The Stoics ask us to imagine ourselves as a dog dragged along behind a cart. We have two choices: to pull and struggle against the rope and try to go in another direction, or to acknowledge where the cart is heading and trot along happily with it, avoiding pain. At times, the cart will truly need re-directing, and we might find ways of doing that constructively. But meanwhile, our anger and frustration, whose ugly passion only obliterates the message we wish to convey, signify our inflated assumptions as to how neatly the world is ready to fit in with our wishes. Lowering our expectations of others is not to let them get away with everything: it is to stop obtruding our stories and priorities on to those of others and then whining when they don't measure up.

When we consider our interactions with others

– such as those in the service industries or, particularly, anyone we employ to make our lives easier – let's imagine that sliver of space where our two worlds intersect as the mutually illuminated portion created by two sweeping searchlights skimming each other in the night. Each of us, grazing only the circumference of the other's private domain, meets the other in a relationship in which our conflicts, pressures – in short, all that excuses our wrongdoing – remains unseen and unsuspected. We perhaps play parts (employee and employer, customer and assistant): roles that are occupied inauthentically and delineated by a fear of our rumbling humanity, which, if it were to truly speak, would threaten collapse. In our more intimate relationships, where our expectations of acquiescence may be greater and the demands we make more pressing, it is particularly important to consider and honour the unseen inner life of our partner, and reassess to what extent they are supposed to meet our expectations. Rather than seek to create a single bond, each lover, wrote the poet Rainer Maria Rilke, should stand guard over the solitude of the other.

No one is on this earth to make our lives easier.

IT IS NOT A CRISIS

Events, as we have seen, act like a trigger, which precipitates an unconscious process that in turn leads to an eventual behaviour. Something happens, and we form a judgement in response. The first impression of the event is artificially expanded. Perhaps, for example, we feel the dark flutter of anxiety or anger. We apply a set of inhibitions to the process: what sort of response is permissible? In a work or social situation we are likely to respond differently from how we do with our partners. We may have specific rules about what is or is not acceptable. Our mood here is vital: feeling hurried, hungry or tired – especially if we have not identified that we are acting from such a deficit – will make us irritable. And at the end of all this, we exhibit our response.

A particularly helpful inhibition we can apply when we feel fury is to *wait*. If we give it time before responding – before sending that email or rising to the occasion – our anger or panic will most likely deflate to a more appropriate intensity. A delay will give us time to take in new information, and prevent us from embarrassing ourselves by making misplaced accusations or exhibiting a fury that we later wish we could retract.

Our Stoic task in the meantime is to avoid adding to first impressions. If we wish our anxiety or anger to be heard, it always helps to cycle back to our first feelings, before we embellish them with fretful narratives and accusations. Where we can remember to do so in the heat of the moment, it serves us to pedal back from, for example, 'You were so rude,' to something like, 'The way you said that made me feel terrible.' By describing only our honest feelings, we avoid the inevitable provocation and escalation caused by involving blame. An accusation is a story on our part, a narration of our interpretation of events, our assumption of their motives. We have played out a scenario in our heads and are now basing our response on that brief work of dramatic fiction. Instead of 'You never listen,' let's aim to offer only the first impression: 'It makes me feel annoyed when you do that, like you're ignoring me.' Own it. Most likely we have been over-sensitive because something has reminded us of how we felt when we were young: unheard, talked over. Treating the feeling as our own means we can now make our feelings known without worsening the situation with accusations that will truly fall on deaf ears.

Some people are predisposed to catastrophise. Life then is lived out as crisis. If our background has encouraged us to be alert to the advent of emergency – perhaps because of a volatile parent – we are going to move to a state of alarm very easily. Our partner has to spend time with an attractive co-worker: clearly, they will fall in love. We have a sore leg: it must be a ripped tendon, or worse. The normal mess of a kitchen triggers alarm because it disturbs a mind eager to keep the world safely in order. A partner's habit of yawning without covering his mouth reminds us of our father, who did the same, and we hate this because it now makes us feel ignored in the same way we did as a child. Our response may baffle those around us, but it always comes from a point of fear. It's a terrible way of encouraging what we really require, which sweetly is only to be heard, to be reassured.

Of course it is near-impossible to direct ourselves *not* to think of things, especially if we have a tendency to do so. To tell ourselves, *this is not an emergency* is unlikely to help us. We have to conjure in our minds precisely what we are supposed to avoid. We need a positive thought to move *towards*, rather than instructions as to what to move away from. In the same way, stopping smoking by *trying not to smoke* is never as effective as *deciding to be a non-smoker*. The Stoic method gives us that positive focus: *Is this thing under my control? In which case, how might it be fine as it is?*

We might also ask: *What are the triggers that lead me to the panic of catastrophe? What advice would I give a dear friend in this situation? How is the situation OK?* Then: *Of what from my childhood do those situations or feelings remind me?*

I recently made the mistake of leaving my dog's toy box on the kitchen table, tipped on one side to be mended, seemingly out of reach of her porcine, bassetty body. While I ate lasagne that night, she, riled by my refusal to share, threw up her front paws, hoisted her considerable heft to the table edge and, in a focused skirmish, tried to extricate from the crate's tangle of mangled animals a squeaky and resistant duck. Three rapid pulls and the favourite fowl broke free, but with it came the entire shaggy menagerie. The plastic box was compelled to follow, toppling upon fat Doodle and causing her to yelp. This was more from shock than pain, as the plastic collapsible box, adorned with Disney Princess illustrations (she chose it herself), was not heavy. But no sooner had that yowl left the sock-wodge of her greedy mouth than she sniffed the air for fallen lasagne and retired with the duck to her bed, where she could both rip out its squeaker and keep watch in case I changed my mind about the food. She had forgotten the accident in a second. She did not replay it to herself, like we replay the scene at the crossing where we were nearly hit by a car, the driver hurling abuse as he passed. She did not form a narrative of resentment: *who left that box there?*; and blamed no one. At the same time, she seems to have learned to be a little more careful of removing objects from the table, or at least she has not tried since. The accident happened and she moved on. The drama left her in an instant, but the sight of it stayed with me.

When we find ourselves worrying or anxious, we might ask ourselves: *Do I have a problem right now?* So much of our unhappiness comes from ruminating over past events or worrying about those yet to come. Where possible, postpone the worry until, if and when the bad thing happens. With events that have already occurred, nothing sustains their power save the tale. Once we strip away the storytelling, we're very rarely in peril.

Shocks to our system like that of the toy box suggest that such (relatively rare) events can disturb us *without* recourse to stories. But the *unnecessary* disturbance will come from their repeated telling, driven by fury, fear of dark potential and the need to find blame. All this perpetuates the narrative of crisis. Be more beagle-basset.

WE ARE NOT SO SPECIAL

Perhaps our greatest failing, the Stoics tell us, is that we keep our accounts badly: we value highly what we have ourselves paid out, but undervalue what has been paid to us.

I never dance at weddings. I hate it, and I am gone long before the horror begins. When I was younger, my reasons for avoiding the dance floor felt complex and sophisticated: to others, no doubt, I was just boring and shy. This contrast of inner experience and outer appearance used to bother me greatly, and were someone to tell me I was evidently insecure about dancing and looking silly, I would defensively splutter something about it not being so simple. We inflict a particularly deep wound when we reduce another's individuality with such conventional vernacular.

If the encouragement to set goals is unhelpful, another way the self-help industry can miss the mark is through their implication that we are each enormously deserving and profoundly special. The stories that support our sense of uniqueness are perhaps the ones we cling to most of all, as they dictate our sense of reality, the way we look out upon the world. But they are over-inflated. We can reduce the pressure — and our propensity to anxiety when those fictions feel threatened — by reminding ourselves, from time to time, of their pomposity. Our opinions are usually borrowed, formed from inadequate information, dispensed to make us seem virtuous. Our tastes are disappointingly generic, our jokes often miss the mark. People talk about us behind our back in the same way we talk about others: our patterns are predictable and prone to parody. Our very sense of self — which we imagine is most deeply our own — is disarmingly malleable and susceptible to the behaviour of those around us. We are, after all, human.

When we are criticised, we grow defensive in a way we would find laughable if we heard it from others. We feel a burst of unbecoming panic, as our flaws (real or perceived) are brought to the light. Something in our evolutionary wiring alerts us to the fear of exclusion: weakness may cast us from the tribe. But in truth, admission of vulnerability is precisely what makes us appear strong. For a moment, it allows those who hear it to relate to us, to recognise their fears and inadequacies in ours, and to know that their faults are normal. To acknowledge a criticism – even an insult – without defensiveness, perhaps even building upon it at one's own expense, can be very disarming. Charisma – and with it true power – rarely emerges from a swaggering play of status.

The vulnerable admission undercuts a dynamic inherent in almost all social interactions. Normally, we endeavour to maintain an impressive appearance while keeping from view a faulty inner world we know only too well. It is the equivalent of an Instagram feed that curates our most picturesque moments into an exhibition of success, while in reality we remain bereft and struggling. The habit is so natural that we forget others are playing the same game. Thus we make the mistake of comparing our clumsy, messy *inner* life with their (usually polished) veneers: an off-target comparison that will rarely make us feel good. Their achievements seem well deserved, whereas ours are surely accidents or sure signs that we are an imposter. We do not see the same labour, failure and self-doubt that have plagued the luminaries to whom we compare ourselves so damagingly. But when we are allowed a glimpse of their suffering, through their self-effacing remarks and emotional honesty, we feel connection and validation. Hence it is vulnerability that creates bonds, and rarely our attempts to be impressive or funny.

One of the greatest methods of minimising inter-personal disturbance is to remind ourselves – with the rich depth of certainty – that we are as flawed and intolerable as the people we are encountering. We cause pain every day to those around us, even when we believe we are acting faultlessly: how much worse is the situation when we are diminished by hunger or lack of sleep? Or when we are acting defensively, because we feel we are under attack? How foully do we behave when, yet again, our attempts to get on with some task have been obstructed by the irritating and minor demands of others? We are capable of every odious behaviour we see in these people, and would act the same if we had found ourselves in their position, with their same history. To meet the minor negligence and incompetence of others with bafflement and irritation is a flagrant denial of empathy: a stance that denies humanity and grossly underestimates the far greater pain we are likely to exert, in total, upon the world ourselves.

We are all struggling to navigate through life without embarrassment. High self-worth is immaterial, and those who display it the most may be feeling it the least, as they shore up their reserves against a world that threatens to topple them. We are not special: we are *similar*, connected by the things that make us feel the most alone, each struggling, each deserving of sympathy. Let's be sceptical of the cry to value ourselves more, for fear we build a toughened case around such a rare jewel. Instead, let it be enough to gather ourselves afresh as often as we can, to take stock of ourselves, in order to greet the world with kindness and a sense of inner unity.

YOU ARE STUCK
WITH YOURSELF

Two awkward aspects of our relationship with desire obstruct the pathway to its satisfaction. The first is this: *the joy we feel in anticipation of a reward almost always exceeds the pleasure of receiving it.* Choosing the spec of a new bit of kit, ordering and awaiting its arrival, taking receipt of the package and opening the box ... this is where all sweetness is to be found for the gadget lover. Our level of happiness may spike for a short while when we obtain something new or begin a new project, but shortly thereafter it is obliged to return to whatever has been established over time. The things we want will make very little difference to how happy we are. And so it must be: if our satisfaction persisted, we would lack the motivation to move on in life, to survive.

This is the hedonic treadmill. The Ancient Greeks were acutely aware of it, though the term was first coined in the 1970s and later developed by psychologist Michael Eysenck in the 1990s. It refers to the cycle of desire fulfilment ('hedonism' means 'the pursuit of pleasure'): we want something, we perhaps get it, we feel good for a brief period and then return to whatever default level of happiness or sadness we enjoyed before. Nothing really changes.

We can extend this thought to the steps we might take to heal the problems of a relationship. Having kids, obtaining dogs, moving house, opening up the relationship to new partners; we can mix things up for a while, but such measures will not sustain the hoped-for feeling of satisfaction.

Regarding the things we purchase, we might start to summon a gentle note of scepticism towards the external things we expect to make us happy, reserving a particular indifference for those luxuries which the marketing industry assures us we direly need. Generally speaking, the more difficult it is to procure something, the less we need it. Unless we are in the direst of situations, the things we do truly need tend towards the plentiful and available. Meanwhile, the currency of advertisers is anxiety. They create a feeling of deficit – *here are the advantages of the latest model!* – to foster in us a residual worry that we are missing out. We can only alleviate that anxiety through acquisition. Thus the more we are able to identify and prioritise what is *truly* important to us, the less we will be pestered by the onslaught of the extraneous. What are the activities that allow us the most peace, productivity, pleasure? Are there things we require to do *those* things well? Do we need to bother quite so much with the others?

The second reason why our normal aspirations rarely provide us with the happiness we hope for is: *you always take yourself with you.* Socrates gave us the following note of caution, which we might remember when planning a holiday:

> Why do you wonder that globetrotting does not help you, seeing that you always take yourself with you? The reason that set you wandering is ever at your heels.

Alain de Botton's *The Art of Travel* expands on this theme. Holiday destinations never quite live up to the glossy promises of their websites, because once we arrive we realise *there we are*, looking out of our own eyes, with our inner life in tow. Ethan Hawke's character Jesse, in Richard Linklater's 1995 film *Before Sunrise*, offers the following words on this theme:

> It's just, usually, it's myself that I wish I could get away from. Seriously, think about this. I have never been anywhere that I haven't been. I've never had a kiss when I wasn't one of the kissers.

You know, I've never gone to the movies, when I wasn't there in the audience. I've never been out bowling, if I wasn't there, making some stupid joke. That's why so many people hate themselves. Seriously. It's just they are sick to death of being around themselves.

Viva variety, rest, sun, recuperation, change and new perspectives. But let's be wary of seeking solutions in new destinations, whether geographical or metaphorical. A new city, a new house, a new partner: we will still be there, with our reliable clusters of unconscious energy, ready to respond to similar triggers as before. When considering making these kinds of changes, it's worth remembering the differences won't be as stark as we might hope. Our level of satisfaction will settle into whatever it tends to be. When it is a better quality of dialogue with ourselves that we truly need, relocation will not change our nature or alleviate our heartache.

AN ALTERNATIVE
TO MEDITATION

If you reach for your phone first thing in the morning, set it in an unusual place tonight before bed. Let this remind you on waking to take two or three minutes to engage in a little *pre-meditation* regarding the day ahead.

As you lie there, you might wish to consider the following thoughts:

I will meet people today who will in some way let me down. They will act like this because in that moment they will know no better. But the wrong they do is similar to my own that I commit every day, just as convinced I am acting fairly. And if I can avoid being dragged down by them, I will be of better service to myself and the world.

Think ahead to challenging situations that are upcoming and, with the advantage of a warm duvet, rehearse some considered responses. From a place of comfort, get ahead of the game. Where, today, are we in danger of letting ourselves down, and acting in a way that we would later regret? What are the alternatives that we can mentally practise now and more easily employ when the time is right? Do we need to utilise the reserve clause – are we setting ourselves up for a fall? Demanding too much of others? Working with unrealistic expectations? Can we lower them? How might it be absolutely fine if things don't go as planned? How much would it truly matter if the contract isn't secured, the meeting turns out to be unsuccessful, or the annoying loudmouth continues to act as he always does? Does having less demanding assumptions about how perfect our partner's behaviour should be, and acknowledging responsibility for our own emotional responses, help clear the murky waters of last night? How about imagining how we would really feel if we lost them altogether? Might that remind us what we value about them? Can we imagine a more admirable way of handling reliably tricky situations?

It may be a conversation we know we must have with a superior. The shy object of our crush who we hope likes us but frustratingly says so little. Our partner or spouse, who yesterday evening embarrassed us over dinner with friends; an event which triggered an argument in the car on the way home and a miserable night without intimacy of any kind. Consider it, think it through, find the best response now, as you are unlikely to discover it in the heat of the moment. What would be generous, balanced, unassuming, dignified – in short, us at our best?

All this serves us far better than beginning our day at the mercy of the digital rabble, brains still spongy and soaked in semi-sleep.

If this morning routine eludes you, consider an alternative: the evening retrospective. Take a few minutes as you sink into slumber to review how you acted during the day. Not to blame yourself for any wrong; instead, to consider new responses for next time: once rehearsed, they will take less effort to conjure.

If we could be bothered to practise both these morning previews *and* evening reviews, considering best approaches ahead of time and later holding ourselves to account, we would live and breathe these Stoic principles far more effectively than a person who merely brings them half remembered to mind when it is already too late. It sounds a lot of work. It might, though, start with just a thirty-second reminder to be the best person we can be, to not attach our emotional well-being to things outside of us, to watch out for known trouble spots, to see tonight if there's anything we should change tomorrow.

REHEARSE LOSS

In 2012 I made a show for Channel 4 called *Apocalypse*. Steven, a young man who by all reports took what he had for granted, became the unwitting participant in an enormous hidden-camera experiment in which the family and life he knew were taken away from him. The point was to rekindle his appreciation for them both. After a period of controlling his news sources, and having his friends and family play their parts, we had him believe the world was about to end through a collision with a huge meteor. Our sequence of pyrotechnic destruction played out during a fateful coach journey, after which he was put to sleep (he had been chosen for his high levels of hypnotic susceptibility). He awoke in hospital, seemingly alone in a post-apocalyptic world. His subsequent journey through our zombie re-envisioning of *The Wizard of Oz* had him discover the qualities of courage, selflessness and decisiveness that he lacked, and ultimately taught him to value that existence to which he had previously paid little attention.

We remember that the Epicureans, whose ideas chimed in several ways with the Stoics', told us: *learn to desire what you already have, and you will have all you need.* How might we desire what we have already? We can do that by loosening our grip on ownership. We can remind ourselves that this thing, this person, is not ours, and certainly not ours for ever.

The Stoic teacher Epictetus gave us some extraordinary advice:

Remind yourself that what you love is mortal, that what you love is not your own. It is granted to you for the present while, and not irrevocably, nor for ever, but like a fig or bunch of grapes in the appointed season; and if you long for it in the winter, you are a fool ... Henceforth, whenever you take delight in anything, bring to mind the contrary impression. What harm is there while you are kissing your child to say softly, 'Tomorrow you will die'; and likewise to your friend, 'Tomorrow either you or I will go away, and we shall see each other no more'?

It might strike us as morbid and unnecessary. Perhaps this is a matter of degree: fixating upon the mortality of our children or the transience of most friendships would bring its own form of anxiety and defeat the Stoic purpose. Yet an occasional reminder of how lucky we are to have the gift of these relationships in our lives surely does us good and shows us how we might come to desire what we already have. This can only come from considering the sobering thought that they must one day come to an end. If we knew these treasured relationships would last truly for ever, would trip and dance through the Garden Immortal and never die, what effort would we make to sustain them, and for how long? Why value time spent together when you have infinite repetitions ahead of you? Would you still fall asleep with interlocked forms and whisper 'I love you' every night for the rest of time? Would you continue to surprise each other with breakfast on any of eternity's mornings you chose, knowing that the rapture of such activity would be quickly lost in the tiniest flickering instant of infinity's interminable drudge?

Embrace the possibility of loss, and allow it to imbue value into what you already have. Rehearse deprivation, by denying yourself certain luxuries for short periods. Consider, for example, what little conscious attention you paid to the comfort of your bed last night: now compare that to the sweet joy of returning to it after a week straddling the nocturnal potholes and obduracies imposed by a cheap hotel. For the same reason, take time to go without your phone, your extravagancies, even your partner. The ancient encouragement to practise loss works because we love what we have *but we desire what we don't*. Learn to see your partner once again through the eyes of others, think of them not as your own – an interesting application of the loss-rehearsal – and faded ardour will be more easily rekindled.

Incorporating this thinking into our lives encourages us at the very least to express our feelings to those we love *now* while we can, to avoid taking them for granted, and to not regret, when it's too late, that they never knew how important they were to us. And rehearsing loss now mitigates the shock and despair of the authentic experience when it arrives.

'A life without temporal boundaries,' writes the philosopher Samuel Scheffler, 'would be no more a life than a circle without a circumference would be a circle.' Or if you prefer Kafka: 'The meaning of life is that it ends.' Bittersweet transience lends context and value. It is intoxicating in the first six months of love to pledge ourselves for the rest of our lives. It is also brave and deeply caring to accept, at least quietly to oneself, that this may prove untenable, or that a lifespan may not turn out to be the generous stretch of time we imagined. 'Transience value,' wrote Freud, 'is scarcity value in time.'

> Limitation in the possibility of an enjoyment raises the value of the enjoyment ... A flower that blossoms only for a single night does not seem to us on that account less lovely.

In matters of the heart, valuing 'scarcity in time' might encourage the more steadfast kind of love, which esteems the present rather than venerates an uncertain future, and, unlike the inflamed delirium that flickers and wanes, grows only brighter with bounded time.

YOUR PARTNER
ISN'T RIGHT FOR YOU

We are creatures of loss. Our religions talk of separation from the Divine, of falls from Grace, of banishment from Paradise. Such themes prevail because they speak resonantly to our human experience. Our lives begin with loss – of the womb, of the bosom: devastating separations from that 'other' which nurtures us. Our caregivers, meanwhile, must navigate the delicate balance of providing for us whilst at the same time letting us down. They have to teach us that the world will not always supply, while minimising the distress of that important fact. Thus the teaching of our $x=y$, *Aims* vs *Fortune* diagonal starts from the first time we scream and don't get anything in return. This disillusionment, if you can remember back to our beginnings, is the task of the 'good enough' parent, as described by Donald Winnicott. And from these early experiences of bonding and deprivation, attachment patterns form that will serve us throughout adult life.

We live this drama of disillusionment before we are old enough to know how to separate the world into that which is *us* and that which is *not*: knowing no better, we believe we are the cause and end effect of every loss and advantage we feel. The traumas and feelings of powerlessness around this time will commonly leave us with some highly charged sensitivities towards feeling abandoned, or feeling engulfed. Resonant psycho-dramas like these are played out repeatedly in our later relationships as we then grow into adults.

Thus if we easily feel abandoned, we may well search frantically for a partner who will nurture us, while we remain prone to jealousy and terror at the first whiff of disconnection. So we seek to confirm our experience of rejection, to replay this childhood pattern again and again, pursuing familiarity above all else; our suspicions and need to control gently, continually, causing partners to withdraw. This repetition is oddly comforting, although it will undoubtedly cause us pain. Enduring a series of such relationships is a way of reinforcing our image of how the world works.

Those of us whose foremost fear is that of engulfment, on the other hand, know the panic of powerlessness that comes when we feel too many demands are made upon us. Some might aim to fight and kick their way out, with a fierce ambition that knows no end, or again, demonstrate a proclivity to control relationships. A common alternative, to which your author is prone, is to adopt a strategy of avoidance: a deft dodging of any conflict or drama that might impinge on the comfort of one's jealously guarded space. Along with this urge frequently comes a leaning towards excessive courtesy, a reluctance to voice one's views, and the presentation of a pacifying, agreeable personality. One's own character is subsumed in favour of avoiding friction, being liked, perhaps of healing others, of bearing too much responsibility. One might seek relationships where the partner can be treated as puppy-like, or needs looking after, so that a comfortable reinforcing dynamic might be maintained. For some, this heightened aversion to intrusion is a common reason for withdrawing from intimacy.

The greatest demand we make of our partner is that they conform to these needs of which we ourselves are only dimly aware. Our unconscious demands are the devils in the darkness, banished from the clearing, expunged from the story we tell of ourselves. They are, by virtue of being unseen, precisely the types of forces that can come to own us. Which is why we can diminish their power only by bringing them into the light, by introducing them gently into the story, into consciousness. Until then, in its shadow form, our nascent fear of powerlessness obtrudes into the dynamics of our relationships with the very people we profess to love most.

As we approach another and offer our hearts, we have an insufficient template in place for love. It is created by the early experience of our parents, who in some ways loved *too* much to set a helpful blueprint for the adult experience (they cooed over us, provided for us, cleaned up after us in a way we should not expect from a partner) while in other ways left us with this legacy of impossible requirements, sore spots and sharp edges. These are our scars from enduring separation in the particular way we did, and we like to pick at them. They call on us to repeat what we knew. Furthermore, when we are older, our first experiences of falling in love are likely to prove formative and embellish these idiosyncratic needs. For example, if our first love is unrequited, furtive and obsessive, we may well seek out the comfort of replication, and maintain a curious preference for the unattainable.

The task we place upon our beloved, to be right for us, is for them to *love us in the way we knew*, or *hurt us in the way we were used to* and, above all, *spare us the difficulty of growth*.

Hoping our lover will be right for us, we recreate them in our image. This is what we're up to when we see them as The One. Or what we do when we avoid any romantic relationships at all because our standards have been set too high. The fantasy of the Perfect Other is defined by our history and enhanced by mystery. The mystery in question is a mixed-up articulation of a lost hope for transcendence we have inherited from the purple aspirations of the nineteenth-century Romantics, who would have us subsume ourselves in the ecstasy offered by a union with perfection. Even less helpfully, we now presume we are to marry someone for love (and a love that will burn for ever). This also turns out to be something we've got into our heads only over the last century or so. A million love songs still sell us their notion of overripe deification and do nothing to advise us where we most need help: namely, how we must navigate the stark domestic realities of a relationship in which, even in the best scenario, we must disappoint and wound each other against our backdrops of personal pain.

As we respond unconsciously to a person's mannerisms or features that happen to occasion echoes of our past experiences, we place our peculiar fantasy on their shoulders and await their compliance, without explaining what we expect. They revive in us a latent cluster of charged sensitivities, triggering our peculiar set of personal associations. These have nothing to do with this individual, but we project them on to him or her nonetheless.

Talk of this kind of projection always brings to mind an image, which I have carried for years. It is the giant 'hologram' of Laurence Olivier's head from the ill-received eighties stage spectacular *Time – The Musical*. In fact, the technological contrivance and

focus of the show's marketing efforts was a mis-
nomer: the effect of a super-sized, floating hologram
was created by projecting a film of Olivier's talking
face on to a giant, solid, white mould of his head. Or
a head, as I don't know if they approached the late
Baron with the request of a cast. No doubt, need-
ing to be elevated or protruded through a star-cloth
from backstage, the head would have been a thing
of lightweight construction and stuck on the end of
a stick. I never saw the show, but when the trick was
explained to me by a classmate I was captivated by the
notion of what an animated projection on to a blank
face would look like. Would the mouth seem right
when it moved? What about the peer's conspicuous
chin: whereupon would the projection settle when
the jaw dropped to speak? A spin through YouTube
does not yield footage from the show but offers more
recent efforts to achieve the same trick: the illusion
is certainly effective despite the chin problem. And
I am sure the effect was captivating for the tourists

and children who came to the repurposed Dominion Theatre and forgave some inclement sneers from the press.

As we project our version of the beloved across their features, we are, in a strange twist, only seeing aspects of *ourselves* in them. If this person is able to render *us* as a blank mould and project just as effectively in our direction, the feeling will be requited, and we might call it love. Both parties are engaged in an optical illusion that may change the course of their lives.

Our task, as partners, is to allow the projection to fade. To permit the revealed other to move and think and talk for themselves. To experience them as truly separate, rather than as a white polystyrene head on a stick fabricated to guide us, according to our script, back to familiar, familial territory. And we can only release them from our projections by asking: *what are the recurring patterns that connect my relationships? What is it that I am expecting of them, that it is not their job to give; what is that thing that I am to now find within myself?*

And why should we bother? We may even wish for a life alone, but then we choose to crustate: to live *solus* is to develop a hardened shell, to deny ourselves the elasticity and growth that are only offered with relationships. As we navigate a genuine connection with a person, they can lead us *forward* to become fuller versions of who we should be. It can be painful to shed one's illusions, to realise that one's partner is not there to comfort, reinforce and restore. With that dawning comes the knowledge that we had lived out a projection, and this is the only means by which we can relieve those we love of our unachievable demands. We can recognise those projections at work when we sense that certain situations cause in us an excess emotional charge, one in truth issued by the rumblings of our history.

To achieve this, it helps to see our partners as there to help us grow. Those points where we clash, once we've got over our defensiveness, might be precisely the areas we need most help. We need help because our relationship to others has had a faulty start, and it will be through healthy, mindful connections that we will be gently guided over time to a fuller sense of self. When they can stand minimally encumbered by the weight of our biography, it will be others who will help us with our task of developing into richer renderings of who we are supposed to be – a process Jung called *individuation*. To allow these people their otherness is not an easy thing, but it represents perhaps the truest calling of love, which is to desire the other to be, to grow. To stand as the guardians of their solitude.

Our partners aren't right for us, because they are not *for* us, and they will only become truly beneficial by being released from the responsibility of providing what we want. Freed in this way from our demands, allowed to be more fully *other*, we may find we each have so much more to give.

A LIFE WORTH LIVING

I

When all is said and done, will we have lived a life worth living? Will we have been present at its centre, or an observer at the periphery, someone along for the ride?

Bronnie Ware, an Australian nurse working in palliative care, recorded what she perceived to be 'the top five regrets of the dying', in her book of the same name. They were:

1. I wish I'd had the courage to live a life true to myself, not the life others expected of me.
2. I wish I hadn't worked so hard.

3. I wish I'd had the courage to express my feelings.
4. I wish I had stayed in touch with my friends.
5. I wish that I had let myself be happier.

Now, we can forgive ourselves if our current priorities don't match those we will later wish we had: it is natural for our needs to be different when our life still extends brightly before us. It makes no sense to live each day as if it were our last: *the needs of a present that has a future are different from one that does not.*

Death rarely rounds off a life with the satisfying ending of a novel or a film. It does not 'complete'; it curtails. It may be no more than an absurd stoppage. If we have the opportunity, it is up to us to bring the story to a close by recognising it as such. And if a person knows she is dying, I would suggest that she needs from her loved ones every opportunity to take stock of her story and bring it to a meaningful end. Despite the fact that those of us who must watch them deteriorate are just doing our painful and miserable best to deal with the situation, it remains better for everyone that a dying person's story is given priority, and not those of us, the onlookers. Our experience is likely to be benefited too, if the deceased is able to leave with as much closure as possible.

If you are facing your own death, and have the clarity of mind and opportunity to make choices, then realise that for you to *own* your death, to author it and to shape it, is tremendously important. You are the protagonist *and* the author. If you do not insist on this central role, you may find yourself reduced to a mere cameo. Others, stronger in body and in number, may take the leading role if you do not. Your death does not belong to your family, or your doctors. They will have their important parts to play, but it is, I think, of ultimate importance that you insist, firmly and sensitively, and through discussion with everyone else, that your choices must steer the process.

Often around death, a conspiracy of silence descends,

and dying becomes very, very lonely. Unwilling to upset or burden those she loves, the dying person does not speak about her fears to her family and friends. Horrified at the thought of saying the wrong thing or appearing to 'write off' their dying beloved, the living do everything to avoid mentioning it in return. In the place of the myths that once guided us through the stopping points of the human journey, a new modern narrative is imposed as we approach our destination: that of the 'brave battle'. This tale, in truth designed only to keep the living happy, tends to further alienate the person facing death. Moreover, it can take her further from experiencing the extraordinary richness of that final time that only a measure of acceptance can bring. As cancer ate through her spine, a friend, Debra, wrote to me:

It is also unhelpful to be told enthusiastically to 'keep fighting, don't let it beat you' or, most annoyingly, 'don't give up!' All that these inane, positive yet totally inappropriate comments do is to make the sufferer (me) feel they are lacking in moral fortitude or backbone (which I quite literally am nowadays). The insinuation is therefore that my current predicament is, somehow, my own fault. Taking an honest and authentic look at my situation, and in so doing, accepting that I am going to die, does not equal giving up, it means I don't waste time over petty things – life is too short, especially mine!

We might never rid ourselves of a lingering anxiety regarding our death; this is a kind of tax we pay in return for self-awareness. But, as with any fear that becomes inappropriately inflated, we can, like Debra and many others, learn to stare it in the face when it comes. With further thought, we might even elevate our lives by gently accommodating ourselves to it right now, before it threatens to become urgent and terrifying. Rather than a dreaded stranger, Death may become a companion of sorts. Perhaps uniquely amongst the objects of our dread, death instructs us how to live.

11

Will our life have been the one we wished to have? In a thousand ways, invariably not, because our plans tend not to work out, despite the snake-oil promises we were offered along the way. Hard-nosed ambition won't do the trick: it is more likely to later count as a regret. So is a life guided by an urgent drive to fix problems. The Stoic approach is effective for ensuring greater levels of tranquillity, and perhaps for most of the time, that's likely to be enough.

But not all of the time. The Stoics tell us to 'remove disturbances', but for some this might come to mean merely 'hiding away safely' where nothing can harm them. This is a meagre substitute for flourishing. Our recommended aim then is maybe *not* so much to be happy, as to live fully and make sure we are moving *forward*. The poet Rilke suggests 'imagining an individual's experience as a larger or smaller room ... most people are only acquainted with one corner of their particular room, a place by the window, a little area to pace up and down'.

Wholeness cannot be found in the mere avoidance of troubling feelings, however helpful the tools of the Stoics are for reassessing attachments and finding one's centre of gravity. To live without anxiety is to live without growth. We shouldn't try to control what we cannot, and we must take responsibility for our feelings. But the reason for this is to walk out into the world with strength, not to hide from every danger.

If you feel anxiety, try letting it sit. See if it is amenable to the lessons we have learned from the Stoics. Use the techniques of this book to divest anxiety of its excessive force. Settle securely into the truth that you do not need to mend what is outside of your control, and you will lessen its potency. When it persists, you do not need to *fix* that too: the compulsion to rectify, to control, is what fuels the anxiety in the first place. Anxiety, claustrophobia, panic: these are feelings *that you have*; they are therefore not *you*. Ultimately, they will pass, and prove amenable to a change in mood or circumstances, because life is largely a succession of short-lived affairs, one matter after another, each giving way to the next. Rather than seeing anxiety as the enemy to be feared, you might even welcome it as a guest.

So while we treat these ideas as a means to a more tranquil life and an antidote to the *unnecessary* disturbances that carry us away, perhaps the pangs of ordinary anxiety might be a good thing. Why would we not wish to pay attention to these agitations, if they have something to teach us? Anxiety is a signal that we are not in harmony with ourselves. Who is? It is good to detach from worthless sources of worry, but also vital for our flourishing to listen to those rumblings and see from whence they arise. Of what does this disturbing feeling remind us from our past? What fear lies half hidden behind this dread? What part of myself am I closing off? Why is this obviously important?

Very few people find the right partner without the pain of breaking up with a previous one. We don't change our career for the better without first letting our current job get us down. Few of us start anything new without the pain of ending the old or the frustration of enduring it. Disturbance can be a signal that we are moving in the right direction: namely, out of our comfort zone. To remain tranquil and comfortable would deny us our growth. To remain happy would stop us flourishing. We can manage our anxiety in the ways we have discussed, but when it stirs, it is likely to be a helpful sounding from an untended part of us that wishes now to be heard. If we shut our ears to these voices, they will come in time to own us, because only the things that remain unconscious are truly in charge. Jung called them 'offended gods', by which he meant energy-charged aspects of our personality (such as the erotic, the creative, the aggressive) that, if not honoured, will wreak their revenge. They are the monsters, lurking in the dark, excluded from the fire-lit clearing where stories are told.

The final call, then, is not to merely seek tranquillity, but from its protected shores, to welcome its opposite. It is a strong society that encourages dialogue with its enemies, and a fearful one that promulgates reductive nouns and categories to demonise and circumvent the unsettling complexities of untidy reality. We, too, must seek the same conversation within ourselves. And do so before the forces we repress rage against us.

We do not need to fear the world, or treat it with suspicion. Any monsters that dwell there are our own.

LIST OF SOURCES

Arthur Schopenhauer, *Counsels and Maxims*

Seneca, *Letters from a Stoic*

Epictetus, *Enchiridion*

Sigmund Freud, 'On Transience in the land of Goethe'

Lines from *Before Sunrise* written by Richard Linklater and Kim Krizan, 1995, for the film produced by Castle Rock Entertainment and distributed by Columbia Pictures

WITH THANKS

To my editor Susanna Wadeson at Penguin Random House, to Andrew O'Connor for suggesting a shorter, handier version of *Happy*, to the Piglace for letting me write and teaching me so much, and to Doodle for our stolen weekends.